Annalopé Cafe – Lisa Kinney & Majel Gardzelewski

D1132621

In memory of our sister, Eloise Kinney, who was always an inspiration to us with her knowledge and expertise in the literary field as a book reviewer and to our mother, Phyllis Poe Kinney, Ph.D. At age 99, she maintains a sense of humor and deep understanding of human strengths and foibles from years of being a mother, grandmother and counselor to many.

Annalopé Cafe – Lisa Kinney & Majel Gardzelewski

Annalopé Cafe

By

Lisa Kinney

&

Majel Gardzelewski

Annalopé Cafe – Lisa Kinney & Majel Gardzelewski

Annalopé Cafe – Lisa Kinney & Majel Gardzelewski

ISBN: 978-1-914130-68-7

Annalopé Cafe – Lisa Kinney & Majel Gardzelewski

Annalopé Cafe – Lisa Kinney & Majel Gardzelewski

OTHER TITLES BY IMPSPIRED

Out of the Chrysalis –
by Mary Farrell

Periodic Stories V3 -
by Jim Bates

Rattlesnakes and Flattops –
by Mackenzie Thorn

Lily -
by Karl Diaz

Irish Hares & Seahorses –
by North Coast Writers

Classical Adaptations –
by Susie Gharib

The Spiritist –
by Theresa C. Gaynord

Annalopé Cafe – Lisa Kinney & Majel Gardzelewski

Contents

Alive in the Spirit	1
Death Separates	3
Gammi Poe	5
Class of 2020	7
Pastoral Symphony	9
Yellowstone	11
With You	13
Fur Elise	15
Alike	17
Hope in 2020	19
Ventricular Tachycardia	21
B.J's Answer May Have Been a Joke	23
Blind Arms	25
Remain, Ukraine	27
How to Serve	29
Assurance	31
Annalope Café	33
Fence	35
Envisioning	37
Encounter in Italy	39
In Trust	41
For Allen	43
Memories	45
East Berlin	47
Praise You	49
Teach	51
Winning Ways	53
Acknowledgements	55

Annalopé Cafe – Lisa Kinney & Majel Gardzelewski

Introduction

By Lisa Kinney

I came to appreciate, at a young age, the pleasure of looking. It costs nothing to look. Perhaps because I grew up in a poor family in Wyoming, one of seven children, entertainment wasn't something I connected with economics. I had to amuse myself. Sometimes God provided the entertainment through nature; other times it was inspired by human beings. But I found it wherever I looked, in reflections, shadows, buildings decaying, reflections of windows: a myriad of pleasures waiting for me to see.

Many photographers stage their photos, and occasionally, I do as well, finding a glimpse of myself in a reflection, or the shadow I cast on a scene. My favorite painting is Velazquez "Las Meninas," painted in 1656. He depicts the young Margaret Theresa in a chamber attended by maids, bodyguards, chaperones, and her parents. Velazquez paints himself in one mirror in the room. He also reflects her parents in another mirror observing their daughter being painted. Unwittingly, his painting looks like a modern photograph, with photographer/painter included. I am incorporated into some photos of this book, not always

in plain view, with one similar to the Velazquez
portrait.

The vast majority of the photographs I take,
however, are simple observations framed by a lens.
Often, I will laugh aloud as I see something hilarious
that has seemingly gone unnoticed—humor plays a big
part in my photographs. I love magical sunsets and
imposing mountains, but I'm mostly pulled by the
closer, human-made objects in places where people
congregate, and where they walk by amazing views
daily and don't recognize them. I see the world
differently and try to capture the odd view—the
common oddity.

Introduction

By Majel Gardzelewski

I am often inspired to write about the beauty, fragility and endurance of life. While being quite personal, my poetry includes many common themes that I believe to be relevant and compelling enough to share with others. It is paired here with my sister, Lisa's often surprising and nuanced photography, from which I have taken both inspiration and motivation to write accompanying poems. I feel that they differ from ekphrastic poetry, in that they are not always directly related to the photograph, but are rather reactions, emotional or intellectual, to what was viewed. "Ekphraisis" a term first used in 1715, is defined as "a literary description of or commentary on a visual work of art." c 2022 Meriam Webster, Incorporated.

Alive in the Spirit

This aging grows hard,
like bricks fade and crumble,
sunsets dissolve
in seconds.
Once I felt immortal,
young as the world around me,
invincible;
but the building that houses me now
is no longer sturdy or supple.
It has a will of its own
and gives in
to entropy and weariness.
Yet I
am being renewed,
learning lessons,
 living by faith,
reaching out
to give and accept
what I can
of life's best.

    M.G.

Santiago de la Compostela, Spain - 2007

Death Separates

Death separates us.
Agonizing grief, alone,
now serenity

L.K

Shirley Basin, Wyoming - 1977

Gammi Poe

My grandmother washed dishes
for us seven kids and Mom.
Her feet wore holes
in linoleum by the sink.
Gammi never wasted any time.

M.G.

Annalopé Cafe – Lisa Kinney & Majel Gardzelewski

Laramie, Wyoming – 1977

Class of 2020

How did we pass that year?
Many suffered, many more died
than we could agree upon;
how did we pass those days,
with masks and mandates,
banned from businesses,
 barred from nursing homes,
careers and degrees
down the drain,
blindsided by fear, futility.?
We did our best; amazingly,
we pulled through,
but what awaits us
when we crawl
out of our sleeping bags?

M.G.

Fort Collins, Colorado - 2020

Pastoral Symphony

Much beauty exists
unseen by mankind;
we occasionally catch a glimpse.
The Creator on high
is an artist and musician,
whose works fill the earth
and inspire imitation;
through gifted hands,
His feats continue on.

M.G.

Ferry Falls, Isle of Skye, Scotland - 2014

Yellowstone

Tourists and photographers,
birders and biologists,
hikers, bikers, writers,
foreign born employees,
families with children
come to view a vast array
of creatures in their habitats;
grey wolves, red foxes,
grizzly bears and cougars,
bison, elk, bull moose,
bighorn sheep and mountain goats,
marmots, beavers,
seen with love and healthy fear,
curiosity and awe.
Visitors are greeted
with reluctance and reserve;
what can the animals sense
of man's intentions??
Untamed, misunderstood,
they share the earth with us;
they feel the pain
and know the joy of living.

    M.G.

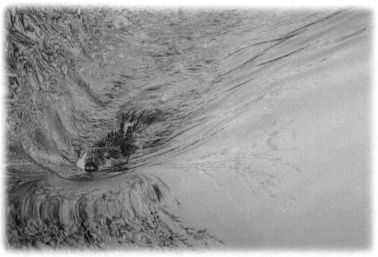

Wyoming - 2019

With You

Fifty years is too long
to remember
life without you,
though I knew
I was home when we met
and you melted my heart.
We traveled through storms,
over mountains and seas,
with kids and then grandkids;
I held fast,
in courtrooms and classrooms,
hospital rooms,
giving birth,
receiving a heart.
Fifty years is too short
a time to share my life
with you;
for love has no end.

M.G.

Annalopé Cafe – Lisa Kinney & Majel Gardzelewski

Bennington, Vermont - 2021

Fur Elise

for Eloise

We loved you, little sister,
(big to Flippy,)
mother, daughter, aunt and friend;
we will not forget
the happiness
of all our times together.
Losing Bill and
 wasting sickness
took a terrible toll.
Your body failed,
your spirit followed;
 we lost you.
No one could match
 the singer, poet, writer,
loving, steady
source of inspiration
that you were.
May the Keeper of the universe
hold you.

M.G.

Annalopé Cafe – Lisa Kinney & Majel Gardzelewski

Laramie, WY - 1980

Alike

Oblivious of
clouds dancing above their heads,
antelope frolic.

M.G.

Sybille Canyon Road, Wyoming – 2017

Hope in 2020

Thursday night, July 30

The Red Sox won the game
to the delight
of cardboard cutouts.
Was performance for the
cheering sections only?
Dashed hopes pervaded,
but some rose
to the occasion;
True mettle beamed
in lives of men and women
and their fans.

M.G.

Red Sox/New York Mets game – 2020

Ventricular Tachycardia

We all have days
 of climbing the walls,
searching for things to do.
The need to find purpose
can lead to
daring creativity
or frustrating futility;
shoveling snow on the roof,
which would it be? not useless,
but truly not wise.
I recall when Allen,
who had an implanted
 defibrillator,
was up on the roof
cleaning leaves from our gutters.
Alerted by a powerful jolt,
he managed not to fall
and came down.
Later, he was knocked to his knees
after exiting a courtroom.
The small device
served its purpose when
as he watched a movie end,
it shook him to the core
and saved his life.

    M.G.

Turpin Meadow Ranch, Wyoming – 2022

B.J's Answer May Have Been a Joke...

"I've been contemplating the destruction
of all the evil in the world."
This doctor of psychology
had been in prison camps
for the duration of the war;
he knew the depths to which
humanity can go.
He didn't smile a lot,
was tough to know,
but in his words I find
a glimmer of the future,
a time when good will overcome
and earth be filled
with peaceful, loving souls,
as things were meant to be.

M.G.

Edinburgh, Scotland – 2014

24

Blind Arms

Arms behind my back,
following dullards blindly-
Putin's evil war.

L.K

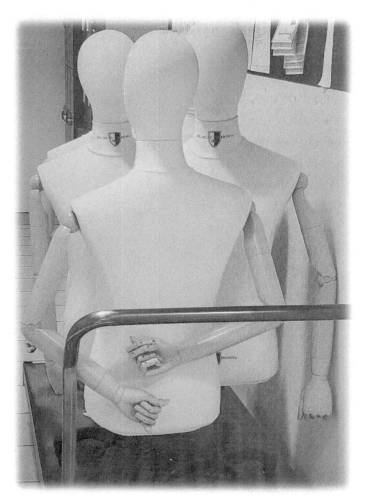

Calgary, Alberta, Canada – 2022

Remain, Ukraine

Open wounds
 and war scars,
the stalk is gone-
enemy missiles and bombs
left only roots.
Fight on, brave souls;
your faith inspires!
Stay strong, dear friends;
for aid will come!
Cry out! Injustice
will not conquer;
you will thrive!
Remain, Ukraine!
All we can offer,
are hands and hearts,
 lifted in prayer,
weighed down in grief;
we ask for angel armies.

M.G.

Great Falls, Montana - 2022

How to Serve

In seeking to know God,
there is a difference:
given all we need to live in peace,
set apart, called to bear witness
to His truth, we have still to decide
how to serve as followers,
like sheep or sharers of the yoke
He shoulders.
Is it how we walk
in fullness of the Spirit,
how we bare our hearts,
submit, petition, love?
In knowing Him is freedom
to give whatever we choose:
as we wait on him
The potter is the artist
and Father of His works,
we are the clay He fashions,
beloved children,
workers in His fields.

M.G.

Sinks Canyon Road, Wyoming – 2018

Assurance

Ukraine, I feel you are my heart,
bombarded, bombed and blasted
where you stood and fell,
your bloody chambers
filled with crushed hopes,
your children buried
where they should be carried
in love's arms.
Mothers ran and cried out to the rocks
to cover them;
fathers were forced
to finally surrender,
knowing all was lost.
Ukraine, you are the heart of the world,
lying lifeless now;
yet just a spark
will bring your pulse again.
Rest assured

M.G.

Virginia Dale, Colorado - 2019

Annalopé Cafe

I've lived in towns and cities of
this lonely state out west,
where women's rights were fought for,
outlaws laid to rest.
The wild winds and winters
guard its isolation;
it has the fewest (and the finest)
people in the nation.
Bison, deer and jackalope
are often seen at play,
but not enough to keep afloat
the Annalope Cafe.
The lovely parks bring visitors,
though few will stay;
residents of Wyoming state:
"We like it that way."

    M.G.

Annalopé Cafe – Lisa Kinney & Majel Gardzelewski

Lamont, Wyoming – 2015

Fence

Holding back some snow
and sunshine
yielding hues of Wyoming sky
on snowdrifts,
stark photograph
warmed by heavenly blues,
winter's beauty
in a world of woes.

M.G.

Fort Collins, CO - 2021

Envisioning

In the mirror we are backwards,
in the window, slightly blurred;
in the instrument's reflection,
beams the light not seen nor heard.
Life is heavy, full of sorrows;
laughter heals the broken bones;
sweetest music elevates
with its uplifting tones

(Proverbs 17:22-)

M.G.

Calgary, Alberta, Canada – 2019

Encounter in Italy

Placid goat with entreating eyes,
spelling out your plight,
beautiful creature drawing close,
but causing me no fright.
In early morning I awoke
to see you hauled away;
my tears fell freely down,
but there was nothing I could say.
We journeyed on to find the place
my grandfather was born;
my heart was full to learn of him,
but for the goat, forlorn.

M.G.

Argriturismo near Marsicovettere, Italy - 2018

In Trust

Seemingly
knowing someone
does not reveal
their falls or victories,
sacred secrets.
Come to no conclusions;
judge no one,
wait for what is shared in trust
and treasure it.
Truth through others' eyes
is worth the wait.

M.G

Bilbao, Spain – 2007

For Allen

Your gentle touch
affirms me;
your zany wit spreads merriment.
You say
what I am thinking
or we speak together;
our minds have merged,
hearts are entwined.
The strings of love,
tuned by years together,
are producing
harmonies with chords
of fulfillment.

M.G.

Annalopé Cafe – Lisa Kinney & Majel Gardzelewski

Loveland, CO - 2021

Memories

Books and paintings
read and viewed together,
stories,
remembered over time, retold
are colored by experience
and personality;
secrets of the heart
play a part.
Colors seen through
different eyes
are not quite the same.
Is there one true value or
are all perceptions true?

M.G.

Kansas – 2019

East Berlin

What is the force that brings it all together,
things unexplained and full of mystery,
when hope becomes what happens,
random pieces make a whole,
coincidence becomes
an empty concept.
Who is the one that seems to smile
when lost things are found,
miraculous becomes believable?
Love is the power; it tears down every wall.

M.G.

East Berlin Hostel – 2018

Praise You

Praising you for being

Almighty God, for seeing

a world dying hopelessly

and sending your dear Son

to rescue the ungrateful,

idolotrous and hateful.

Your heart was broken, torn apart

crushed by everyone.

I worship you for love's

flames from above

In the person of your Spirit

which empowers me.

Because you first loved me

so unreservedly,

to you I pledge my heart and soul

for all eternity.

M.G.

Edinburgh, Scotland - 2018

Teach

for Catherine

the English language to re-enrollers,
beginning with a simple prefix, re:
revere, to honor those who are worthy;
relinquish is to give up willingly;
repairing could be moving to new space;
religion;
faith and doctrine for the soul;
refurbish is to tidy up a place;
reintegrate;
bring back into a whole.
Restore is to revitalize, revive;
redress is to remedy, set right;
resourcefulness can overcome a problem;
reflection, serious thought;
remorse, hindsight;
reiterate, repeat for clarity;
recuperate, relax and get some rest.
What is the relevance of using words like these?
Simply rewording something may be best.

M.G.

Laramie, Wyoming - 1960

Winning Ways

Even in the face of angst, calmness prevails
when turmoil tears the soul apart with darts and nails;
grounded on a rock, staunch as a mother bear,
he stands to fight with kindness and sagacity,
weapons used to win wars. The vanquished pales;
The contest never really was there.

M.G.

Norway - 2014

Acknowledgements

We would like to acknowledge Philip White Jr. for his assistance in technology, suggestions and invaluable experience and also Andrea Carlson and Jeanette Gardzelewski for their encouragement and help.

-   Majel Gardzelewski

I would like to thank Shelby Kinney-Lang, my son, for always encouraging me with photography, supporting my slightly off-beat views, and editing my writing. Also, thanks to my husband, Rodney Lang, for stopping the car multiple times in our trips, when I needed to take photos.

-   Lisa Kinney

About the Authors

LISA KINNEY

Lisa Kinney was born and raised in Laramie, Wyoming. She has a BA from the University of Wyoming (UW), in Spanish and education, and a minor in German. She received an M.L.S. from the University of Oregon, and a J.D. from UW. She spent a year studying Chinese in Scotland at the University of Edinburgh. She was director of Albany County Public Library for 6 years; owner of Summit Bar Review, a course teaching law to lawyers taking the bar exam; a partner with the law firm of Corthell and King; and a financial advisor with AIG/VALIC. She was the 6th woman to be elected to the Wyoming State Senate and served as Minority Leader during part of her 10 years as a Senator.

She wrote a book on lobbying, published by the American Library Association and co-authored several books on the civil rights of individuals with mental illness and developmental disabilities for Wyoming Protection and Advocacy. She and her brother Bob Kinney hosted a photography exhibit at the University of Wyoming entitled 'Ashes to Ashes' in 2019 focusing on roadkill. Photography has always been Kinney's passion, in addition to her being a mom of three great kids, Cambria, Shelby, and Eli.

Annalopé Cafe – Lisa Kinney & Majel Gardzelewski

MAJEL GARDZELEWSKI

The author received a Bachelor's degree in English from the University of Wyoming, where her studies included poetry classes. The author has retired as a paraprofessional in elementary and middle schools, having worked with children with autism and disabilities in Living Skills classes. Her love for poetry led her to create twenty small books of poetry, stories and photos of her own and of others over several years. In 2017, she and Lisa Kinney self-published a book of the author's poems with some of her sister's photographs in a collection titled: " A Change of Heart, From Self to God." The author chose photographs to illustrate some of the poems she had written, some dating back to the 1970's. For the current book, the author has chosen several photographs of Lisa's and written poems based on impressions that she has got from viewing them. The author and her husband of 50 years, Allen, reside in Colorado, where they enjoy spending time with their children and grandchildren, as well other relatives and friends.